Now I Know

Stars

Written by Roy Wandelmaier

Illustrated by Irene Trivas

Macmillan/McGraw-Hill School Publishing Company
New York Chicago Columbus

For information regarding permission, write to
Troll Associates,
100 Corporate Drive,
Mahwah, NJ 07430.

This edition is reprinted by arrangement with Troll Associates.

Macmillan/McGraw-Hill School Division
10 Union Square East
New York, New York 10003

Printed and bound in Mexico.
ISBN 0-02-274907-1

1 2 3 4 5 6 7 8 9 REY 99 98 97 96 95 94 93 92

It is day.
Can you see a bright star?

Yes, you can!

The sun is a star.

The bright sun is so close to us.

It outshines all the other stars.

Now it is night. Look up.
Look at the other stars.

All the other stars seem small.
That is because they are so far away.

But many stars are bigger than our sun.

They are called red giants.

Some stars are smaller than our sun.

They are called dwarfs.

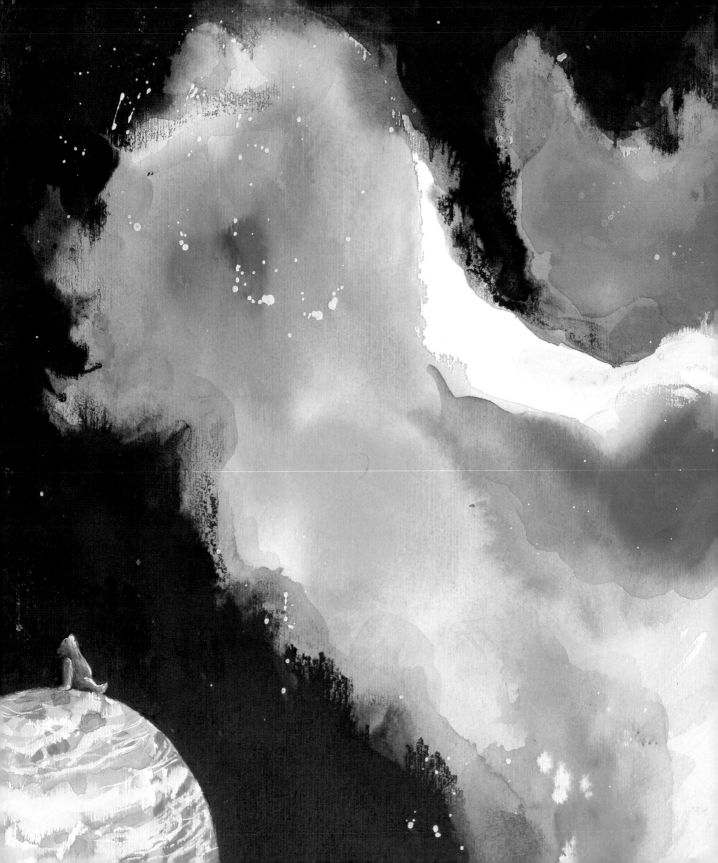

How does a star begin?
When gas and dust in space come together,
a star is born!

Let's take a trip to the stars.

A star glows hot.
A star glows bright.
Are all stars as hot as our sun?

Some are even hotter!

The hottest stars give off blue light.

Cooler stars give off red light.

Our star, the sun,
is not the hottest or the coolest star.
It is in the middle. It shines yellow.

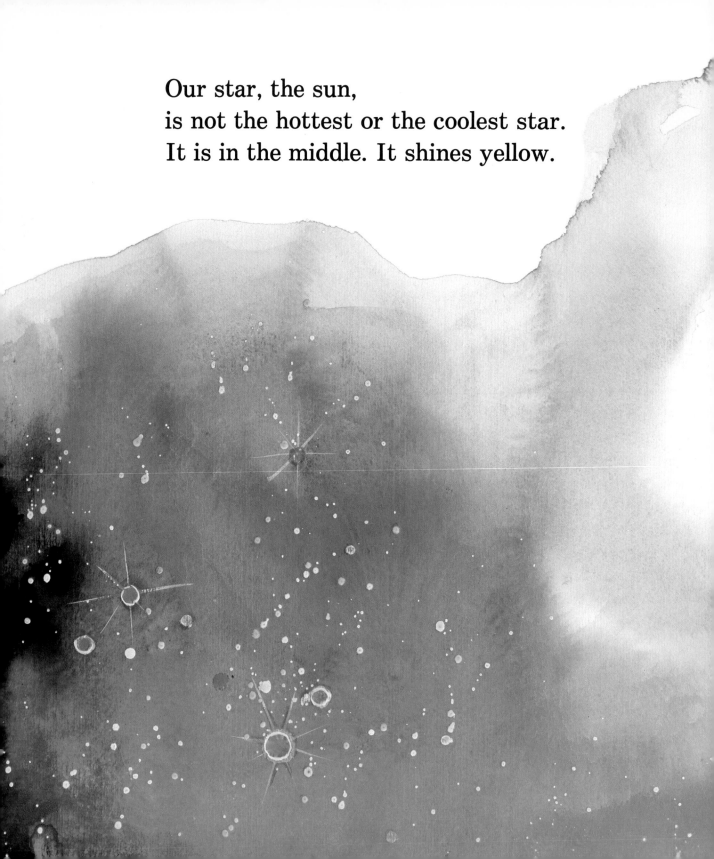

After some stars live a long time,
they explode. We call this a supernova.

The exploded gas goes out into space.
And some of it may be used to make a new star.

Stars are so far away.
But stars are close enough to shine for us.

Watch for them tonight.